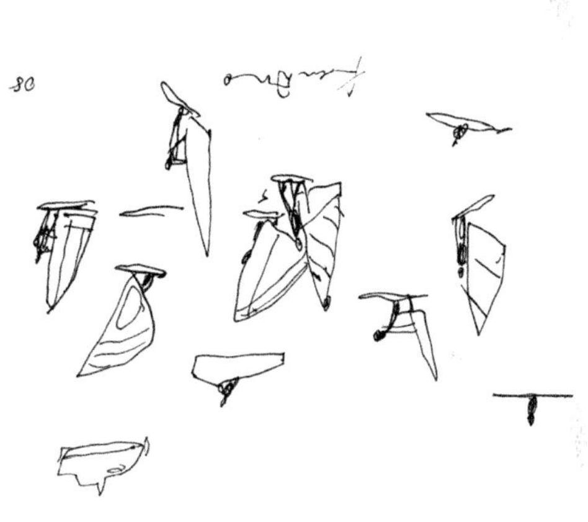

Ken Done

Thames & Hudson

SYDNEY

Sydney

I've lived in Sydney most of my life.
As a teenager, I travelled across the harbour every week to go up, by tram, to the National Art School, having received a special exemption to enroll in 1954. This was before the Opera House was built, and the land was used as a tram shed instead.

I live beside the harbour now, and my gallery in The Rocks is close to both the Opera House and the Harbour Bridge. It is stunning to see them both in a single vista; I never tire of it and I've made many works to show their relationship.

Sydney is undoubtedly one of the world's great cities, much as Sydney Harbour is one of the world's great harbours.

We have travelled to cities around the world, but nothing, for me, will ever beat Sydney.

From little coves to crowded beaches, it's a growing metropolis that has learned to protect the past.

I love it.

KD

Sydney, 1980

Sunset at Clontarf, 1980

ontarf
Ken Done
80

Big rock, 1987

Two rowing boats, 1991

Boats and red hibiscus, 1991

The Wednesday Race I, 1980

The world-famous musician James Morrison is an old friend. He once released an album of music inspired by a number of my paintings.

In one song, he gave a musical notation to the way I had placed my drawings of yachts in this work, The Wednesday Race.

Who could ask for more? KD

Saturday sailing, 1984

Leaving the Heads, 1992

Yachts and freighters, 1992

Boat reflections, 1991

Coloured Sydney, 1985

The wind dropped, 1992

May 2, 1992

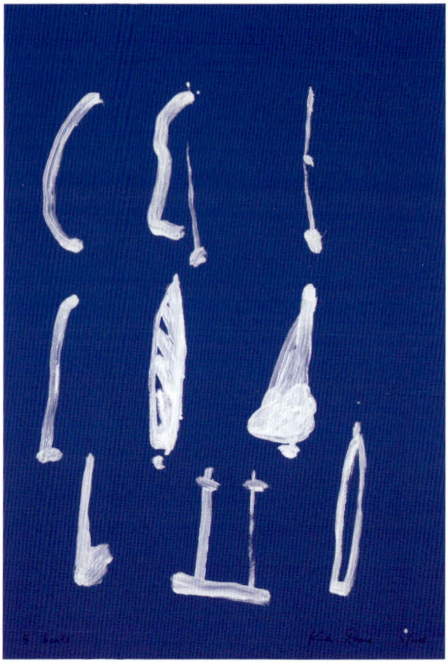

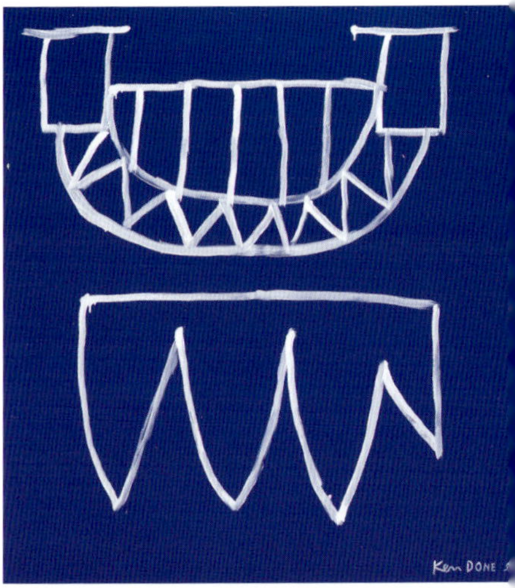

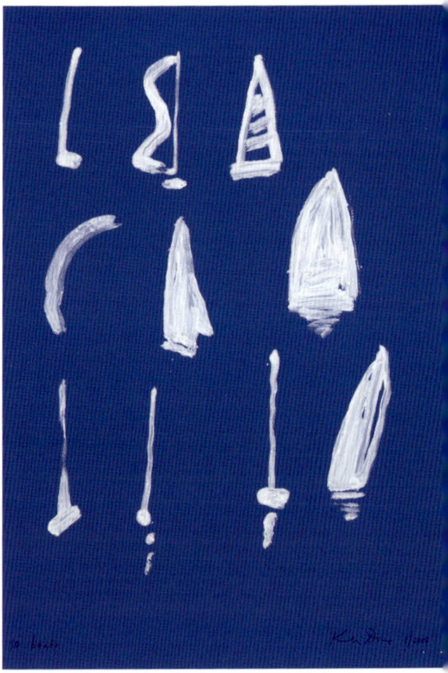

9 boats, 1988
Bridges, 2001

Sydney Down Under, 1993
10 boats, 1988

White Opera, yellow sky, 1998

Sydney Harbour, turquoise sea, black liner, 2001

Sydney night, three-quarter moon, 1996

Sydney by night, 1995

Sydney night, half-moon, 1996

Sydney Harbour, eastern suburbs II, 1998

Sydney Harbour, eastern suburbs III, 1998

Sydney Harbour, eastern suburbs IV, 1998

Eleven boats, 1998

The Bridge and the House I, 1998

View to the Bridge, 2008

Opera House, waving to the Bridge, 2001

1 *Harbour*, 2001

Bridge, boat and green sea, 1998

I love the pattern of the
steel girders on the bridge,
and the shape of the stones
that make the pylons.

And then the huge bulk
of a cargo ship as it
heads out to sea, seen
through the delicate sails of
some Sydney Harbour yachts.

KD

Chequered sail, 1999

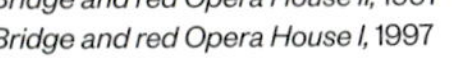

Bridge and red Opera House II, 1997
Bridge and red Opera House I, 1997

These works simplify
the Harbour Bridge and the
Opera House into the most basic
shapes and colours.
In them, I used the actual grey
paint that workmen use to
continually paint the bridge itself.
It seemed the best way
to get the perfect colour.

KD

Bridge and red Opera House IV, 1997
Bridge and red Opera House III, 1997

Uluru and Kata Tjuta.
Ayers Rock and the Olgas.
Icons that, with a little imagination,
are the same shape as the
Opera House and the Harbour Bridge.
How amazing they all are.

There works explore the use of
indigenous dots and stripes,
incorporating them into the great icons
of the Bridge and the Opera House.
I've painted these two so many times,
and these works are examples of the
games I play graphically with them.

KD

Bridge IV, 1996

Bridge VI, 1997

Bridge I, 1996

Bridge II, 1996

Bridge III, 1996

Opera House, yellow and red sea, 1999
Bridge, bird, Opera House, sun, 1999

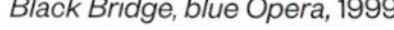
Black Bridge, blue Opera, 1999

Bridge and six parrots, 2000

Orange hibiscus and a grey green sea, 1999

Late evening, Blackwattle Bay, 1999

Floundering on the rocks I, 2001

Container ship, 1999

Late light, city from the west, 1999

Sydney night, white birds, 2000

Easter Sunday morning, 2010

Palms and gulls, 2001

Pink sail, 2001

Yacht club, 2003

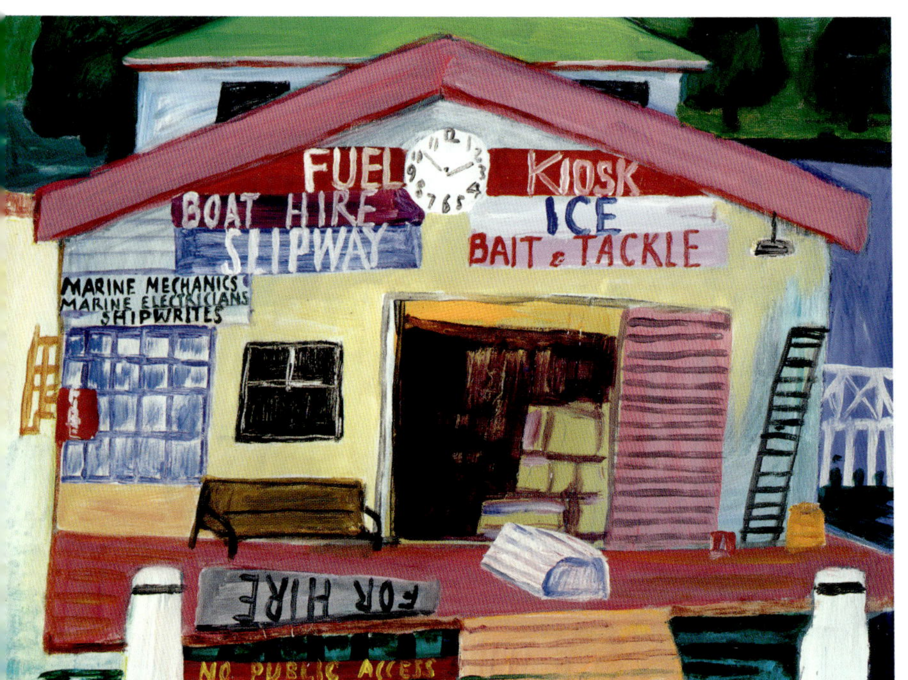

Boat shed, 2002

Fishing at Manly, 1992

Opera House, new moon, 2001

Sydney Harbour, spotted Opera House, black sky, 2006

Sydney Harbour, striped Opera House, green sea, 2006

Bridge and Opera House by night I, 2003

Balmoral moon I, 2004

Night Bridge and emerald sea, 2003

Sydney Harbour afternoon, 2003

LASER Light on
the
Ken Done 18·1·2004

Laser light on the Opera House, 2004

After Amad Jamal, 2004
Sydney late afternoon, 2004

Hot day on the Harbour, 2019

Dangerous rocks, 2004
Balmoral late afternoon, 2004

Chinamans surf boat, 2003

Looking at yachts in the changing light, 2005

Bougainvillea hanging over our little wooden gate.

This spot has been an inspiration for a lifetime of painting.

One day, when I was 14, I walked around the rocks from Balmoral to Chinamans Beach.

I was stopped in my tracks by a little overgrown house tucked into the corner of the beach.

Many years later, the Cabin became my studio, and we still swim and breakfast there every day we can.

Most of the moored yachts have gone now, but I always loved the one in this painting, with its blue hull and turquoise-green sail cover.

KD

Bougainvillea and blue boat, 2005

Chinamans Beach, November I, 2005

Chinamans Beach, November V, 2005

Pelican morning, 2007
Kayaking with the orange dog, 2009

Balmoral boats, 2006

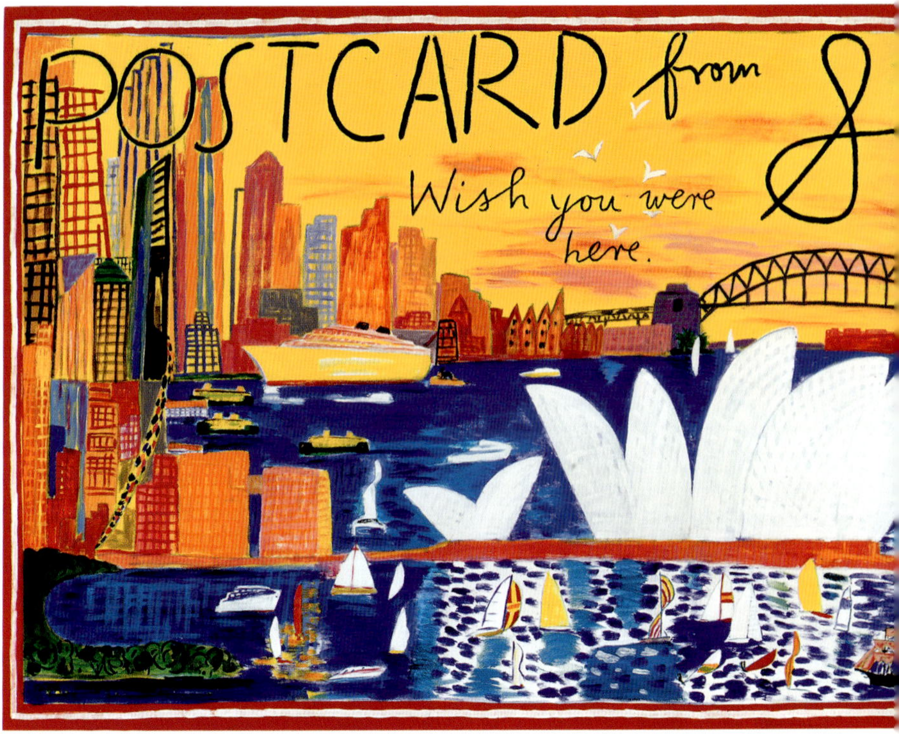

Postcard from Sydney, 2002

Postcard from Sydney, blue Sydney, 2007

Opera House and the Bounty, 1996

Pale emerald sea, 2007

Postcard from Sydney, September, 2007

Postcard from Sydney, 2018

Sydney dreaming II, 2007

Sydney dreaming, 2007

Outback Bridge and Opera House, 2007
Sydney Harbour night, 2007

Sydney yellow sky, 2007

Sydney sailing, 2007
November afternoon, 2007

Blue Sydney, 2007
Sydney, mauve sky and striped sea, 2007

Walking to work I, 2009
Walking to work II, 2009

Walking to work III, 2009
Walking to work IV, 2009

Looking at the Opera House, 2009
Opera House, black sea, night sky, 2009

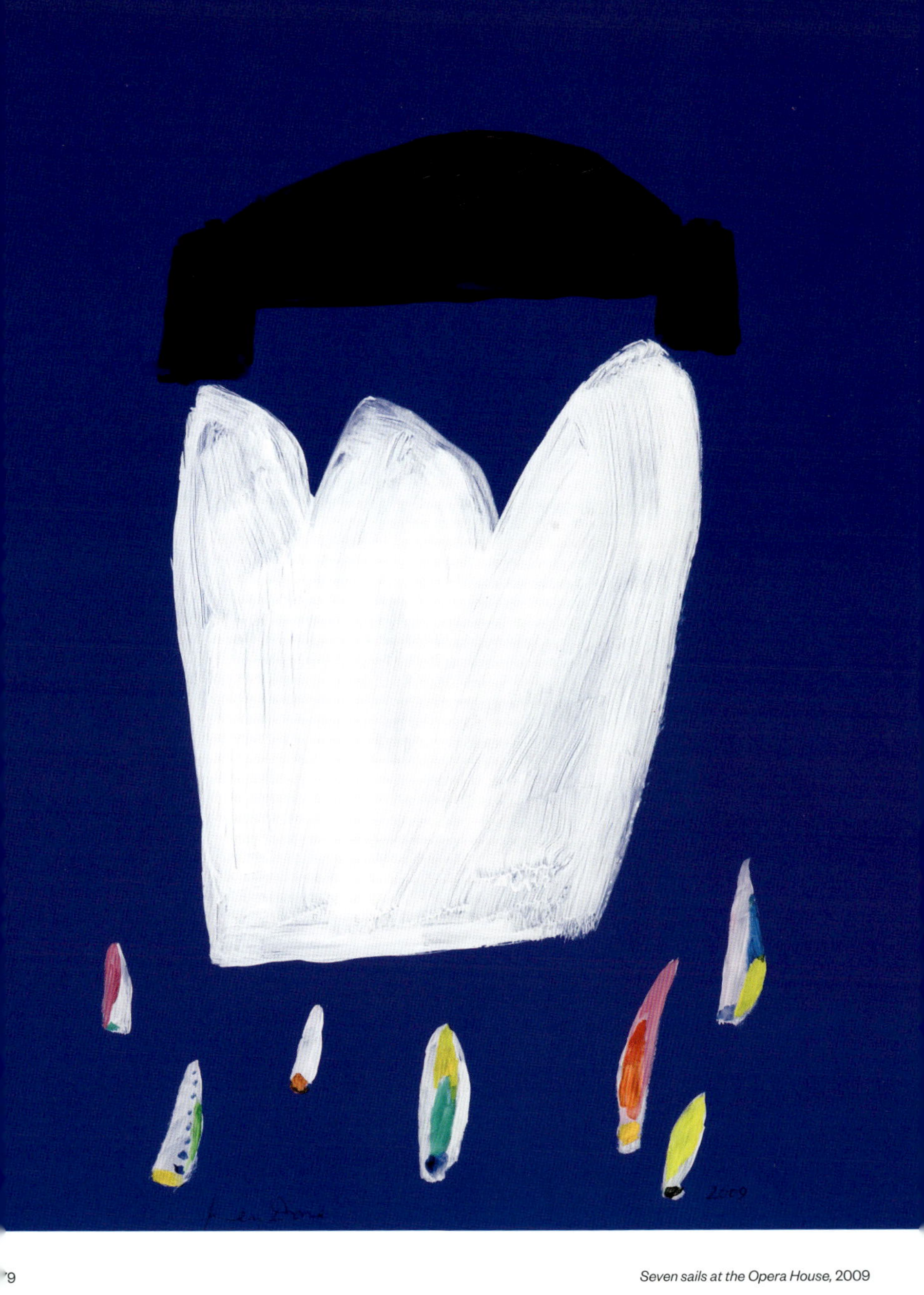

Seven sails at the Opera House, 2009

Magpies at the Opera House, 2008
Flowers and city, 2013

How wonderful that a city should be symbolised by an opera house. I've played so many games in paint with its glorious shape.

Opera House palette, 2009

It can be the song of a magpie
early in the morning, a huge
bunch of flowers or
the palette of a
playful painter.

KD

Sydney Harbour, chequered sea, 2011
(opposite) *Mauve Opera House, green clouds*, 2011

Sydney February I, 2007

Early light I, 2002

Early light II, 2002

Balmoral seagull I, 2011

Opera House and Palm Trees

Opera House and palm trees, 2012

Beach and sailing, 2014

Sydney Harbour, pink sky, yellow sea, 2014

Glancing at the kayaks, 2003

Balmoral, blue cloud, blue sail, 2014

Saturday sailing, 2016

Opera House in May, 2015

Pink Opera, 2015

Postcard from Sydney, yellow spotted sea, 2016

Postcard from Sydney, pink Opera House, 2016
Bridge walk II, 2007

Postcard from Sydney, grey sea, lilac sky, 2016

Windsurfer on a mauve sea, 2017

Boats and yellow freesias, 2014

Opera House and ultramarine Bridge, 2019
Opera House and cadmium orange Bridge, 2019
Opera House and Luna Park, 2019

Opera House, watermelon sky, 2019
Opera House, emerald sea, 2019
Opera House, lilac sea, 2019

Opera House, lilac and blue sky, 2019
Opera House, Prussian blue sky, 2019
Opera House, violet sea, 2019

Opera House and red ferry, 2019
Opera House, green sky, green sea, 2019
Opera House, burnt orange sky, 2019

Pink sea, 2019

Rocks, 2019

Sydney celebration, 2007

ABOUT THE AUTHOR

Creative, optimistic and bold, Ken Done's work reflects the vibrant heart of Australia and Australians. Drawing and painting since boyhood, he has been chronicling the Australian landscape for decades, but it wasn't until his fortieth birthday, in 1980, that he held his first exhibition. Since then, he has held more than fifty solo shows, including major exhibitions in Australia, Europe, Japan and the USA. The recipient of an Order of Australia for services to Art, Design and Tourism, Ken Done's paintings are held in collections throughout the world.

LIST OF WORKS

1 Windsurfers
2008
Pen on paper
10.5 x 15 cm

2–3 Postcard from Sydney,
Wish you were here
2015
Ink on paper
30 x 42 cm

7 Sydney
1980
Oil crayon on paper
58 x 45 cm

8–9 Sunset at Clontarf
1980
Oil and acrylic on canvas
78 x 96 cm

10 (top) Big rock
1987
Oil on board
61 x 51 cm

(bottom) Two rowing boats
1991
Gouache on paper,
34 x 30 cm

11 Boats and red hibiscus
1991
Acrylic on canvas
101 x 76 cm

12 The Wednesday Race I
1980
Oil crayon and ink on paper
42 x 33 cm

13 Saturday sailing
1984
Oil on canvas
55 x 43 cm

14 Leaving the Heads
1992
Acrylic and oil crayon on canvas
46 x 61 cm

15 Yachts and freighters
1992
Acrylic and oil crayon on canvas
46 x 61 cm

16 Boat reflections
1991
Gouache on paper
47 x 64 cm

17 Coloured Sydney
1985
Oil crayon on paper
37 x 45 cm

18 The wind dropped
1992
Acrylic on paper
58 x 77 cm

18–9 May 2
1992
Acrylic on board
71 x 92 cm

20 (top left) 9 boats
1988
Acrylic on coloured card
68 x 48 cm

(top right) Sydney Down Under
1993
Acrylic on canvas
225 x 200 cm

(bottom left) Bridges
2001
Acrylic on canvas
213 x 152.5 cm

(bottom right) 10 boats
1988
Acrylic on coloured card
68 x 48 cm

21 White Opera, yellow sky
1998
Acrylic and oil crayon on clayboard
61 x 46 cm

22–3 Sydney Harbour, turquoise sea,
black liner
2001
Oil, acrylic and oil crayon on canvas
61 x 76 cm

24 Sydney night, three-quarter moon
1996
Acrylic on canvas
152 x 122 cm

24–5 Sydney by night
1995
Acrylic on canvas
153 x 119 cm

25 Sydney night, half-moon
1996
Acrylic on canvas
152 x 122 cm

26 Sydney Harbour, eastern suburbs II
1998
Oil and acrylic on board
61 x 76 cm

27 (top) Sydney Harbour,
eastern suburbs III
1998
Oil and acrylic on board
61 x 76 cm

(bottom) Sydney Harbour,
eastern suburbs IV
1998
Oil and acrylic on board
61 x 76 cm

28 (left) Eleven boats
1998
Oil crayon on paper
35 x 27 cm

(right) The Bridge and the House I
1998
Oil crayon on paper
35 x 27 cm

29 View to the Bridge
2008
Oil crayon on paper
34 x 26 cm

30 Opera House, waving to the Bridge
2001
Oil, enamel and acrylic on canvas
213 x 152.5 cm

31 Harbour
2001
Oil, enamel and acrylic on canvas
213 x 152.5 cm

32 Bridge, boat and green sea
1998
Acrylic on coloured card
51 x 41 cm

33 Chequered sail
1999
Acrylic and oil crayon on paper
57 x 76 cm

34 (top) Bridge and red
Opera House II
1997
Oil and acrylic on canvas
91 x 76 cm

(bottom) Bridge and red
Opera House I
1997
Oil and acrylic on canvas
91 x 76 cm

35 (top) Bridge and red
Opera House IV
1997
Oil and acrylic on canvas
91 x 76 cm

(bottom) Bridge and red
Opera House III
1997
Oil and acrylic on canvas
91 x 76 cm

36 Bridge IV
1996
Acrylic on canvas
122 x 152 cm

36–7 Bridge VI
1997
Oil, acrylic and enamel on canvas
172 x 218 cm

37 (top left) Bridge I
1996
Acrylic on canvas
122 x 152 cm

(top right) Bridge II
1996
Acrylic on canvas
122 x 152 cm

(bottom right) Bridge III
1996
Acrylic on canvas
122 x 152 cm

38 (top) Opera House, yellow and red sea
1999
Acrylic and oil crayon on paper
57 x 76 cm

(bottom) Bridge, bird, Opera House, sun
1999
Acrylic on paper
57 x 77 cm

39 Black Bridge, blue Opera
1999
Acrylic on paper
54 x 76 cm

40 (top) Bridge and six parrots
2000
Acrylic on card
50 x 82 cm

(bottom left) Orange hibiscus and a grey green sea
1999
Oil crayon and gouache on paper
58 x 76.5 cm

(bottom right) Late evening, Blackwattle Bay
1999
Acrylic and oil crayon on paper
37.5 x 56.5 cm

41 (top) Floundering on the rocks I
2001
Oil and acrylic on canvas
80 x 100 cm

(bottom left) Container ship
1999
Acrylic and oil crayon on paper
37 x 57 cm

(bottom right) Late light, city from the west
1999
Acrylic on paper
36 x 51 cm

42 Sydney night, white birds
2000
Oil, acrylic and enamel on canvas
150 x 120 cm

43 Easter Sunday morning
2010
Oil and acrylic on canvas
122 x 152 cm

44 Palms and gulls
2001
Oil and acrylic on board
36 x 46 cm

45 Pink sail
2001
Oil on board
60 x 76 cm

46 Yacht club
2003
Gouache and oil crayon on paper
30 x 42 cm

47 Boat shed
2002
Acrylic on clayboard
46 x 61 cm

48 Fishing at Manly
1992
Acrylic on canvas
76 x 101 cm

49 Opera House, new moon
2001
Oil on canvas
44 x 51 cm

50 Sydney Harbour, spotted Opera House, black sky
2006
Oil and acrylic on canvas
92 x 122 cm

51 Sydney Harbour, striped Opera House, green sea
2006
Oil and acrylic on canvas
91.5 x 122 cm

52 Bridge and Opera House by night I
2003
Oil and acrylic on canvas
150 x 120 cm

53 (top) Balmoral moon I
2004
Oil, acrylic and enamel on canvas
122 x 91 cm

(bottom) Night Bridge and emerald sea
2003
Oil and acrylic on canvas
40 x 51 cm

54–5 Sydney Harbour afternoon
2003
Oil and acrylic on canvas
120 x 150 cm

56–7 Laser light on the Opera House
2004
Oil and acrylic on canvas
61 x 91 cm

58 (top) After Amad Jamal
2004
Oil and acrylic on canvas
61 x 91 cm

(bottom) Sydney late afternoon
2004
Acrylic on board
46 x 61 cm

59 Hot day on the Harbour
2019
Oil and acrylic on linen
152.5 x 122 cm

60 (top) Dangerous rocks
2004
Gouache and oil crayon on paper
30 x 40 cm

(bottom) Balmoral late afternoon
2004
Acrylic on canvas
80 x 100 cm

61 (top) Chinamans surf boat
2003
Oil and acrylic on canvas
40 x 51 cm

(bottom) Looking at yachts in the changing light
2005
Acrylic on canvas
80 x 100 cm

63 Bougainvillea and blue boat
2005
Oil and acrylic on board
61 x 46 cm

64 Chinamans Beach, November I
2005
Oil and acrylic on canvas
40.5 x 50.5 cm

65 Chinamans Beach, November V
2005
Oil and acrylic on canvas
40.5 x 50.5 cm

66 (top) Pelican morning
2007
Oil and acrylic on canvas
91 x 122 cm

(bottom) Kayaking with the orange dog
2009
Oil and acrylic on canvas
61 x 76 cm

67 Balmoral boats
2006
Oil and acrylic on canvas
80 x 100 cm

68–9 Postcard from Sydney
2002
Acrylic on canvas
200 x 400 cm

68 (bottom left) Postcard from Sydney, blue Sydney
2007
Acrylic on board
30 x 41 cm

(bottom right) Opera House and the Bounty
1996
Acrylic on canvas
122 x 152 cm

69 (top right) Pale emerald sea
2007
Acrylic on canvas
41 x 51 cm

(bottom left) Postcard from Sydney, September
2007
Acrylic on canvas
76 x 102 cm

(bottom right) Postcard from Sydney
2018
Oil on linen
152 x 122 cm

70 Sydney dreaming II
2007
Acrylic on canvas
150 x 120 cm

71 Sydney dreaming
2007
Acrylic on canvas
150 x 120 cm

72 (top) Outback Bridge and Opera House
2007
Oil on board
61 x 91 cm

(bottom) Sydney Harbour night
2007
Acrylic on canvas
92 x 122 cm

73 Sydney yellow sky
2007
Acrylic on coloured card
68 x 48 cm

74 (top) Sydney sailing
2007
Acrylic on canvas
80 x 100 cm

(bottom) November afternoon
2007
Acrylic on coloured card
48 x 68 cm

75 (top) Blue Sydney
2007
Acrylic on coloured card
48 x 68 cm

(bottom) Sydney, mauve sky and striped sea
2007
Acrylic on canvas
61 x 76 cm

76 (top) Walking to work I
2009
Oil and acrylic on canvas
24 x 30 cm

(bottom) Walking to work II
2009
Oil and acrylic on canvas
24 x 30 cm

77 (top) Walking to work III
2009
Oil and acrylic on canvas
24 x 30 cm

(bottom) Walking to work IV
2009
Oil and acrylic on canvas
24 x 30 cm

78 (top) Looking at the Opera House
2009
Acrylic on card
44.5 x 37 cm

(bottom) Opera House, black sea, night sky
2009
Acrylic on canvas
60 x 70 cm

79 Seven sails at the Opera House
2009
Acrylic on coloured card
44.5 x 37 cm

80 (top) Magpies at the Opera House
2008
Oil and acrylic on paper
50 x 70 cm

(bottom) Flowers and city
2013
Acrylic on canvas
38 x 45 cm

81 Opera House palette
2009
Oil and acrylic on board
45 x 60 cm

82 Sydney Harbour, chequered sea
2011
Oil on board
46 x 61 cm

83 (top) Sydney February I
2007
Oil and acrylic on canvas
61 x 92 cm

(bottom) Mauve Opera House, green clouds
2011
Oil and acrylic on board
45 x 60 cm

84 Early light I
2002
Oil and acrylic on canvas
84 x 102 cm

84–5 Balmoral seagull I
2011
Oil and acrylic on canvas
38 x 76 cm

85 Early light II
2002
Oil and acrylic on canvas
84 x 102 cm

86–7 Opera House and palm trees
2012
Oil and acrylic on canvas board
27.5 x 35.2 cm

88 Beach and sailing
2014
Oil and linen
122 x 91 cm

89 Sydney Harbour, pink sky, yellow sea
2014
Oil and acrylic on linen
152 x 121 cm

90–1 Glancing at the kayaks
2003
Oil and acrylic on canvas
40 x 51 cm

91 Balmoral, blue cloud, blue sail
2014
Oil and acrylic on linen
102 x 122 cm

92 Saturday sailing
2016
Oil and acrylic on linen
122 x 96 cm

93 Opera House in May
2015
Oil on board
41 x 51 cm

94 Pink Opera
2015
Oil on linen
122 x 152 cm

95 Postcard from Sydney, yellow spotted sea
2016
Oil on linen
153 x 122 cm

96 (top) Postcard from Sydney, pink Opera House
2016
Oil on linen
153 x 122 cm

(bottom) Bridge walk II
2007
Acrylic on coloured card
39 x 48 cm

97 Postcard from Sydney, grey sea, lilac sky
2016
Oil on linen
153 x 122 cm

98 Windsurfer on a mauve sea
2017
Oil and acrylic on linen
153 x 122 cm

99 Boats and yellow freesias
2014
Oil on linen
122 x 91 cm

100 (top left) Opera House and ultramarine Bridge
2019
Oil and acrylic on linen
30 x 40 cm

(top right) Opera House, watermelon sky
2019
Oil and acrylic on linen
30 x 40 cm

(left) Opera House and cadmium orange Bridge
2019
Oil and acrylic on linen
30 x 40 cm

(right) Opera House, emerald sea
2019
Oil and acrylic on linen
30 x 40 cm

(bottom left) Opera House and Luna Park
2019
Oil and acrylic on linen
30 x 40 cm

(bottom right) Opera House, lilac sea
2019
Oil and acrylic on linen
30 x 40 cm

101 (top left) Opera House, lilac and blue sky
2019
Oil and acrylic on linen
30 x 40 cm

(top right) Opera House and red ferry
2019
Oil and acrylic on linen
30 x 40 cm

(left) Opera House, Prussian blue sky
2019
Oil and acrylic on linen
30 x 40 cm

(right) Opera House, green sky, green sea
2019
Oil and acrylic on linen
30 x 40 cm

(bottom left) Opera House, violet sea
2019
Oil and acrylic on linen
30 x 40 cm

(bottom right) Opera House, burnt orange sky
2019
Oil and acrylic on linen
30 x 40 cm

102 Pink sea
2019
Oil and acrylic on linen
112 x 82 cm

103 Rocks
2019
Oil and acrylic on linen
112 x 82 cm

104–5 Sydney celebration
2007
Acrylic on canvas
120 x 150 cm

106 Me
1992
Oil and acrylic on canvas with a painted frame
102 x 76 cm

112 Sydney Harbour
2009
Pencil on paper
23 x 17 cm

On the cover:
White Opera, yellow sky, 1998 (see p.21)

First published in Australia in 2020
by Thames & Hudson Australia Pty Ltd
11 Central Boulevard, Portside Business Park
Port Melbourne, Victoria 3207
ABN: 72 004 751 964

www.thamesandhudson.com.au

23 22 21 20   5 4 3 2 1

Thames & Hudson Australia wishes to acknowledge that Aboriginal and Torres Strait Islander people are the first storytellers of this nation and the traditional custodians of the land on which we live and work. We acknowledge their continuing culture and pay respect to Elders past, present and future.

978 1 76076 079 3

NATIONAL LIBRARY OF AUSTRALIA
A catalogue record for this book is available from the National Library of Australia

Design: Evi-O.Studio
Printed and bound in China by RR Donnelley